The Weight
of Numbers

Winner of the Walt Whitman Award for 1987

Sponsored by The Academy of American Poets, the Walt Whitman Award is given annually to the winner of an open competition among American poets who have not yet published their first books of poetry.

Judge for 1987: *Mona Van Duyn*

The Weight
of Numbers

Judith Baumel

Wesleyan University Press
Middletown, Connecticut

These poems, sometimes in earlier versions, appeared in the following publications:
The Agni Review: "Details"; "That First Angelico"
The American Poetry Review: "The *Fruition* of Berneray, Hebrides"
The Antioch Review: "Mary Frank's Bedroom"
The Harvard Advocate: "From the Diary of Juan de Pareja"
Boulevard: "'The Split Bulb and Philandering Sigh of Ocean'"
The Denver Quarterly: "At the Tomb of The Venerable Bede in Durham Cathedral"; "Halfway
There"
Gradiva: "Two Men Loved Me Once"
The Nation: "Speaking in Blizzards"
The New Republic: "To a Friend in Asia"
The New Yorker: "Ginestra"
The Paris Review: "Fibonacci"; "Proper Distance and Proper Time"; "Roches Moutonnées";
"Thirty-Six Poets"
Parnassus: "'The Wild Brother to Whose Hand of Power / The Great Lioness Stalks,
Purring'"
Pequod: "Herschel's Milk"; "The Monk and the Udāyana Statue of Buddha"; "Samuel"
Ploughshares: "Led by the Hebrew School Rabbi"; "Scarborough, New York"
Promethean: "The Child's Room"

"Against The Grain" originally appeared in *Poems: A Celebration,* published by the Newton
Free Library (1982).

The epigraph is taken from Robert Fitzgerald's elegy to Dudley Fitts in *Spring Shade,*
copyright © 1971 by Robert Fitzgerald, and is used by permission of New Directions
Publishing Corporation. The excerpt from "Oysters" from *Field Work* by Seamus Heaney,
copyright © 1976, 1979 by Seamus Heaney, is reprinted by permission of Farrar, Straus and
Giroux, Inc. "The Wild Brother to Whose Hand of Power The Great Lioness Stalks, Purring"
is excerpted from "The Woman at the Washington Zoo," copyright © 1960 by Randall
Jarrell, and is reprinted by permission of Atheneum Publishers, an imprint of Macmillan
Publishing.

I would like to thank the Millay Colony for the Arts, Inc., The Corporation of Yaddo, and the
New York Foundation for the Arts for their generous support.

All inquiries and permissions requests should be addressed to the Publisher, Wesleyan
University Press, 110 Mt. Vernon Street, Middletown, Connecticut 06457.

Distributed by Harper & Row Publishers, Keystone Industrial Park, Scranton, Pennsylvania
18512.

Library of Congress Cataloging-in-Publication Data
Baumel, Judith, 1956-
    The weight of numbers / Judith Baumel. — 1st ed.
       p.   cm.
    ISBN 0-8195-2144-2   ISBN 0-8195-1145-5 (pbk.)
    I. Title.
PS3552.A85W4   1988   87-21180
811'.54—dc19   CIP

Manufactured in the United States of America

FIRST EDITION
WESLEYAN POETRY

For David

And in Memory of Robert Fitzgerald

"What farther land he found I hope to see"

Contents

I

Thirty-six Poets

after Sakai Hōitsu

Some are drunk. Some are mumbling.
Many are solitary, each in his way fixed.
They are all happy over their very good number,
an easy square; its root six,
itself a lovely number, exponential chrysalis.
And if, in the array of patterns
taken from nature—clouds, spider webs, starfish—
we might yet find a true square
not one of these thirty-six, not the one
whose square is on his sleeve or heart, cares.

My old group, my buddies, the Math Team
would measure our drunks by booming
the quadratic formula, gleaming
with rum, slopped over some parents' living-room
rug, like these bards in their curtained cabal.
No one of us flubbed our password,
the drinking song, that poem of radicals
pressed in our brains, no gauge at all, absurd.
Minus b plus or minus the square root of
b squared minus four a c over two a.
Now even sober I lose those cancelled lines of youth
and drunk I am easily distracted, say,
by the discriminant, the bee-squared et al.
Concentrating on minutiae, I am lost in the well-
folded sleeve of the great poet's silk kimono,
lost on the silkworm's trail winding through Japan
and wonder, drunk, watching my steps split by Xeno,
drunk, wonder what led me to the simple numerical plan
and then away like dust in the path of a paper fan.

At the Tomb of the Venerable Bede in Durham Cathedral

Venerable Bede who venerated in their turns Cuthbert
and the many abbots of Wearmouth and Jarrow; Benedict Biscop;
holy King Egfrid; Alchfrid and his father
King Oswiu; Easterwine; Ceolfrid; and Sigfrid,
I venerate you Bede your simple name, your pure loves,
your idea of spiritual growth as three tools of cooking:
the gridiron where we see literally
and in the open, the frying pan where we turn the literal
meaning over and over, the bread oven where we begin
to lay hold in a mystical way
upon what we cannot see yet but hope to see in the future.

We might today venerate others but somehow don't.
The problem is the "veneration," not the who to do it to.
It means nothing though we still have
those things of which Bede wrote. Our Weber grills,
our Silverstone pans, and, for most Americans,
town bakeries, "Silver Cups" churning out steam and nostalgia
beyond our airplane-bothered ball parks.

Here in Durham we have had our only truly good meal in England
and, on the house, a brilliant Châteauneuf-du-Pape.
Old Bede you got squat from the Pope.
Our towel racks warmed up, they served tea in our room,
and we had the best sex of the trip among the crumbs.

We venerate the magnificent Reader's Digest Road Atlas of Britain.
We venerate all the wrong-side passing lanes in this county.
We venerate your stony posthumous cathedral.
We venerate your characteristic graveyards and church doors.
We venerate all our postcards of obsession.

"The Split Bulb and Philandering Sigh of Ocean"

Our shells clacked on the plates.
My tongue was a filling estuary.
—Seamus Heaney

Mussels, clams, scallops, lobster tail and claws,
and a piece of fish
steamed in a Portuguese casserole.
You picked one shellfish, and I, one,
as if from Julia Child's primordial soup
and chewed on those tough strangers
in an empty restaurant.
We attacked the lobster
with a nutcracker and complicity;
a pooled effort of intelligence,
then relaxed
to discover each other secretly mopping sauce
with our bread.

If you had touched my arm then
just to make a point in conversation
I would have thought you forward;
thought so anyway, you were so insistent,
charming, intimate.

Now, in the shallow tide of another sleepless night,
I watch you, recovering from surgery, shift and moan.
Your unconscious noise rattles me—
despite any remedy I offer
the low sound skimming over codeine
does not stop
and the man I assemble piece by piece
to keep me from panic
to tire me into my own loose sleep
is not any more familiar.

What scientists call thinking came late to humans.
Crawling onto the beach
was one thing but when the bones
of our forearm separated at the elbow
and we grasped, flipped our hand,
and brought objects close to our eyes,
our brains learned to analyze, synthesize.

When I hold you I don't touch reason
but accumulation:
each meal's luxurious ingredients,
each day's meals,
day after day of these meals,
your hand in my hand,
everything I want at the end of my arm,
the pieces of bread
we each bring separately to our mouths.

The Child's Room

Down the hall the father
is shaving and his girl watches
from the edge of the tub.
He dabs on a mustache and beard
and pantomimes an old man.
Delighted, the child plays with the foam.
Then the silent, serious shaving—
stroke after stroke wipes his face
young again while the radio
announcer predicts the day's weather.

I could be in the far bed
on the other side of the table
topped with record albums and toys,
the sun making boxy patterns
on the floor and beds.

At night the damask bedspread,
the twill weave of the throw rug,
the pillowcase, the head lamp,
must blend into endless shapes
in the dark room.
Like her stuffed animals,
they become anything
the little girl's fear
imagines them.
Creatures from the stars come in
through the window to carry her away.

And sometime, after an uneasy night,
she may wake late
to the front door slamming,
see her father's suited back
as he walks to the car.

In her sleepiness
she will work furiously at the window
to open it in time
to call, "Daddy, Daddy!"

I used to be startled, roll over,
and face the click of the door,
hear your pants legs
brush together down the hall
those mornings you would sneak out
without touching me.
Now, I wake into this room,
remnants of a childhood,
four walls of flowers.
I stare at that vacant space,
the big window
that I can never open wide enough
or lock perfectly tight.

Speaking in Blizzards

Fifty-two consecutive days of snow.

Brother, I imagine you buried in snow.

The paper reports students jumping from windows
into drifts at the sixth floor.

A character in a current magazine
story says that a man's only female friend
is his sister. His was long dead.

So I phone you, the noise on the line
a fuzz, like snow on a TV screen
and believe I hear the wires under snow,
and see their imaginary criss-crosses
dipping a bit, between the lakes, at Buffalo.

When you answer, "oh, hello,"
a short trailed greeting, I am convinced
that your voice travels through snow
to reach the receiver, that a dense
absorbent snowpack swallows
your message. All I hear is silence,
diffuse, uncomfortable, and I wait for that slow
start of a rivulet when you finally make sense.

It was like this at home.
At the same dinner table, the same school,
we were never quite together, each below
the cramped snow of our house, each alone
for weeks till you'd come sit on the calico
quilt of our sister's bed at night, yawn,
and complain about father, his temper or his rules.

We'd listen, in those late hours, and know
that you would begin the dream-telling ritual,
meticulous details, your plots so logically sewn,
yet somehow a gift you did and didn't bestow.
Your isolated talk: a falling jewel
which parts, then sinks invisibly into, snow.

Against the Grain

Grandma, not a poem about your work;
the tiny stitching of a young girl's hand.
But how, in the best dress shop of a Polish town

you waited for the one man you believed.
In seven years, you knew, he'd leave his mother,
his home, to come to you, to come for you.

From the window of the shop your friends
would watch him pass. A painter. They'd say, "Here comes
your little ladder, Malche." When you married

he stenciled flowers everywhere: the doors,
the kitchen. Went to market in the worst
of winter for fresh milk. To America

beforehand to arrange your second life.
Still, seasick on the boat, your little boy
in mischief, what did you think about? Bad luck?

A stranger, you learned a new way to speak,
how to demand from the butcher a good piece,
how to live for those things closest to you—

your husband and those after dinner walks.
Then years you were alone here, past his death.
Machines in crowded el-train factories

stitched the day, and waking every morning
the eastern light, too light, revealed your room
so absolutely still and empty, hushed.

Now sitting, patient, in a folding chair
by the stoop, a helplessness you grew into,
you will not dare go anywhere alone.

And though you gave his name to me
I live in fear of learning what you know:
that family and landslayt offer warmth

but their absence marks the same old patterned wound.
And while the heart learns to live in solitude
its independence only goes so far.

Details

A particular understanding, peculiar knowledge—
the weaver knows each string of warp;
a comfort of touch. Fingertips
sleying, drawing-in the thread,

the weaver knows each string of warp,
its path and place in the fabric.
Sleying, drawing-in the thread,
each thin piece evolves specific, separate.

Its path and place in the fabric
join with others to form the whole.
Each thin piece evolves specific, separate,
something calm and repetitive,

joins with others to form a whole
as the cook making prune jam—
something calm and repetitive—
repeats each task with regular skill.

As the cook making prune jam
pits and skins the fruit,
repeats each task with regular skill,
warm boiled fruit slips through hands.

Pits and skins. The fruit:
each reward of familiar flesh.
Warm boiled fruit slips through hands
and fingers remember

each reward of familiar flesh
for lovers in a darkened, quiet bed.
And fingers remember
how the body's map of texture changes.

For lovers in a darkened, quiet bed
each velvet hair on the low curve of back,
the body's map of texture changes
to find, perhaps, the zipper of a scar.

Each velvet hair on the low curve of back;
a comfort of touch, though fingertips
find, perhaps, the zipper of a scar,
a particular understanding, peculiar knowledge.

To the Parents of a Childhood Friend, a Suicide

I. *Shelach Lecha / Send for thyself, that they may spy out the*
land of Canaan

To have escaped Hitler and come to this.
What were the gifts that remained to give to her?
Necklaces, pearls, small jewels which she returned
a week before her death? What I remember
is how you'd lie mysteriously silent
and still on the couches in your living room,
the plastic covers on chairs, shades brought down.
The dark and constant eerie presence of blue.
In numbers. And your arms: untouchable
as biblical blue dyes whose formula
and sacred color is lost. I can't explain
this time to you, hunched and thin, alive,
but find I wonder if in "those years" you hoped
to forget you ever ate or slept or kissed.

II. *Massey, Bemidbar / The stages of goings forth,*
In the wilderness

I often feel I catch a glimpse of her
in the predictable streets or find her shape
approaching me in crowds and want to rush
to her to say, "I knew it was a mistake."
But knew, at home last night, I saw for sure,
through open doors, above a pile of clothes,
Emily's white face. Could recognize
a familiar roundness, bits of straight dark hair,
the downward slant of her reluctant smile,
the weight of sadness sitting underneath
her eyes as if some tiny pebbles sewn
in the bags, at birth, steadied and pulled her face,
which, seen, pulls out to our open eyes
dry and hurt with tears that still won't come.

III. *Berit Melach Olam* / *An everlasting covenant*
                              of salt

   Her burial was the second-hottest day
   ever in the city: a hundred and four.
   Only the earth of her open grave seemed cool,
   even sweet. The Rabbi told me privately,
   "we must remember her in life, not death."
   I thought, how wrong, how he could never tell
   one child's unrumpled face from a hurt one
   in school. I bit my hand and tasted salt.
   He'd tell us how conquerors of biblical towns
   spread salt on the ruins, a desert. I remembered how
   Emily forced an extra punishment
   in games of knux. The loser drank two cups
   of warm salt water. No matter if she gagged,
   or, worse, threw up. She drank it all. At once.

IV. *Akedah* / *The offering of Isaac*

   Your childhood disappeared when they changed Lemburg
   to Lvov. When you left the town for German camps.
   And now, once more, when Emily died. Mine too;
   we've lost some recent, private history.
   It's more than convenient talk to say such things:
   the robbery chain-links forever from aunts
   she did not know, past nieces who won't know
   their aunt, and the children who played with you just drift
   into memory from that black unmentioned event.
   Unwilling to be a ram's horn to redeem it,
   my playmate forced me to repeat your loss.
   We're left with nothing. No record of ourselves,
   no bible to measure what has passed or changed,
   and events become just an emblem or a cause.

Proper Distance and Proper Time

Two events have a spacelike separation.
Show that a frame can be found in which
the two events occur at the same time.

All summer he taught relativity
and knew their first time around
they wouldn't understand it
—that intuition of the weight of numbers.
Nothing visual helped:
Explosions on trains.
Twins separated and aging differently.
The pole vaulter running through a barn
so fast the pole shrinks by half
to the size of the barn.
He looked always to one student's squint
and tightened lip, for her form bent
over gas tubes in lab.

At the end they all drove out
to a field to watch the mid-August
meteor shower. He lay next to her
under a college blanket
separate but so close he imagined
the pressure of her knee
through blue jeans melting him.
Then they slept. Her knee as she curled
brushed him and he woke
absolutely still till she shifted away.
In the morning he told her
she was beautiful.
She considered Einstein's paradox:

If I hold a mirror in front of myself
arm's length away
and run at nearly the speed of light
will I be able to see myself?

Scarborough, New York

The slow disengagement
of plaster, wood, brick and concrete.
One layer strips away from another
while ivy that has come up
like a poisonous weed
guards the edge of the wreck.

The remnants of these two walls
take the direct noon lighting,
reflect a brightness which recalls
not the familiar burnt-out
Bronx but a ruin less obvious.

On those roads that run
through slums behind towns
we saw house after house
that might become this one.
Each horizontal plank
sagged unpainted.
Across a front porch clotheslines
weighted with diapers and sheets
described the possibilities
of poverty in small yards
of carrots and radishes
trampled by children on rusty tricycles.

The angle creates an optical illusion
reversing inside and out.
The corner first juts
then folds inward.
A blocked brick window sits too low
facing the wrong direction.

I try to remember our trip
as it was, wet laundry
strung in the back of the car,
the radio stations'
terribly local news,
breakfasts rushed and busy,
always late for days
crowded with detail.

But with this building
I remember most clearly,
like the sharp outlines
of its layered collapse,
the intimations of foundation.

Here things crumble,
play tricks, lead downward.
Curious nails shape long shadows
in the white lower corner
and random grasses
also shadow spindly, abstract.
Detail and lines fall to the bottom,
the shadows and the rubble,
everything obeys gravity,
its natural downward pull.

Fibonacci

for Abraham Baumel

Call it windfall

finding your calculation

come, finally,
to the last decimal point of pi.

In the silence of January snow
a ladybug survives the frost
and appears on the windowpane.

She crawls a tiny space.
Hesitant. Reverses. Forward,
like a random-number generator,
the walking computer frog
who entertains mathematicians.

Think of the complexity
of temperature, quantification
of that elusive quality "heat."
Tonight, for instance,
your hands are colder than mine.
Someone could measure
more precisely than we
the nature of this relationship.

Learn the particular strength
of the Fibonacci series,
a balanced spiraling
outward of shapes,
those golden numbers
which describe dimensions
of sea shells, rams' horns,
collections of petals
and generations of bees.
A formula to build
your house on,
the proportion most pleasing
to the human eye.

Mary Frank's Bedroom

The inviting rumple of her
shadowed bed, at left, the black
deep triangle in the corner
beneath are matched by decorations
on the wall above.

The woman who owns it, played
on this bed,
played the guitar
left across a pile of clothes,
played with their soft flannel,
pajamas twisted between fingertips
and thrown casually on the bed.

Courting me, you once wrote
that you stayed late after a bad party
wandering the house
in your host's expensive things,
his velvet morning jacket
and chinoiserie pants.
You fingered tricky knives
from Hammacher Schlemmer,
pieces of Ming pottery,
all his discreet objets d'art.

I want to slip into this woman's
night clothes,
lift her thin Indian bedspread
unmaking it in one motion—
a moment of billows,
and, the spread's furrows smoothed,
crawl under its shade.

I would imagine you there
all night with me in the dark;
we would play that game
linking pairs of mismatched
words with a stretch of logic
no one else strains or cares for.

Above us swatches of puckered
Indian mirror fabric, postcards, beads,
hang half hidden by darkness.
But details in the cluttered room
can't hold our eye.
Under them we find more:
a crazy-quilt foundation of bricks,
stains, smudges and cracks.

They remind me
of the comfortable, crowded parties
we went to trying to separate.
Both drunk, we'd balance
our way home through alleys,
leaning to rest
against their winter bricks.
And even now I can't call cruel
what I've always known
was somehow cruel:
how you would tuck me in
and leave, gesturing
to demonstrate helplessness.

In all the dark exposure
of this photograph
the oval mirror strikes clear and bright,
mimics the flat light in the Indian fabric.
All white from a window opposite,
they call away from the dark
toward that window we can't quite see,
suggesting a different mystery
in its frightening clarity of light.

A Month in the Country

Is a big mistake.
The demons come out and meet
the terrible sounds of all things approaching
fruition. You discover
the horror of walking out into a perfect darkness
with all your worst dreams walking behind.
Your shoulders ache with anticipation
and though none of your dreams dares actually
extend its strong clammy fist to you
they all creep close.
In the late afternoon meadow you've noticed
ten kinds of irritating grasshoppers,
noting as well your gaze is weak
and untrained, concluding there must be many more,
and just as many annoying varieties of flies.
Oh, abundant minuscule life!
Its multitudes of jeweled butterflies are
every dead soul you've ever known.
I'm sorry, you weep as each one floats past, *forgive
me, I never meant any of it.*

II

Roches Moutonnées

They were the decisive icy fingers
of geology class brought home, stretching
into the parkway.
Soft forms, like yours under blankets now
in that bedroom so far away and so cold
I dream your breath condenses.
That the glacier digs out, at once,
a canal deeper and wider
than the slow shift
of water, its swiftness, appealed,
even though its speed is counted by event,
a one great accumulated thrust,
and not the minutes, years of its advance.
Those remnant rocks on my route home from school,
the ones my childhood friends and I
used for first base or Alpha Centauri in play,
polished and grooved by the cold that changed
them became, one day, mysterious French
sleeping sheep, fleecy stone about to wake.
Oh, the fairy dust of nomenclature
that gave me a moment when
I approached familiar landmarks anew, alert
to new shapes the new metaphor formed,
to how the name transformed susceptible stone.
From then on I gave them my grateful gaze—
there they lay, patient as ever, like you, my love,
writing: *oh, to be sleeping with you, my beauty.*

Ginestra

to Count Giacomo Leopardi

From a distance of reading
a small volume of yours, your Broom,
the desert flower, remained as dry
and flat as its English name suggests.
And your Vesuvius the sterminator, more remote,
as if the green mountain were seen
from a train rushing by in high brutal summer.

Dear Count, the hot, dry, wide streets
of Pompeii offered me no Ginestra,
no nature impervious to our lives, to all
our accumulated, inherited destructions.

No, not there but in Umbria I fully discovered
your flower wildly perfumed, widely
rooted, growing, covering the hills
with so much yellow
Ginestra, Ginestra, over all, random, profuse.

It was the strength of an affection
I'd always had and never known.
This fact. Your poem. Over and over
your words that I hardly believed.
Let me tell you: I was on the back
of a Vespa near Gubbio,
and Ginestra entered my senses
through nose and eyes. A love
I never understood for the friend
driving that Vespa
came back, the way vegetation
will, after calamities,
both slowly and suddenly return.

We may willingly destroy.
We may casually destroy.
We may find nature doing our destruction
for us, but my romantic heart
had escaped to recognize Ginestra
for what it is, the sweet breath of our lives,
Ginestra, powerful presence
of small persistence.

To a Friend in Asia

A long eccentric night
of wrecked sleep:
each hour I wake with
a different loneliness
and I remember how
you talked me through a similar
panicked night last year.
Some unnamable obligation
to keep things together
kept you with me
and talking so late, blurred with affection,
we discovered a new hour
no one had ever seen before.
Touring in Malaysia or Manila,
now, you could be anywhere.
My folded aerograms
disappear to places as meaningful
as the jumble of letters in their addresses.
There are those who don't believe
man ever went to the moon.
The British Flat Earth Society
imagines an American Hoax Theory
and argues we've been deceived
with elaborate models and TV films.
Others say we shattered
some precious dome
bringing rains and permanent disaster.
"Trepidation of the Spheres."
What was Donne's compass metaphor?
He went wandering
and she remained fixed.
Well it is and isn't the same.
With the business of spirits—

no matter where you travel
I'd still hear
your high sympathetic laugh
eager to soothe or entertain;
a thin gold foil,
all that it touches
turning rich and remarkable.
But this should be a simple love letter,
and it is not.

After the 1972 Flood in Elmira

I thought the Mennonites were a colony
of the diseased, like lepers.
They sponsored the relief effort
that bused us first
to a twenty-bed hospital for tetanus shots
before we dug all day in a first-floor parlor
that had maroon roses on wallpaper
staining brown with the sewage
I was hauling
as an old lady who hadn't left town
stared out her third-floor window
across the street.
She was protecting seventeen cats
and I thought if she lived
in one hundred years of solitude
she'd be Amaranta Buendía, black bandage
on one hand, sewing a magnificent shroud.
Instead her perseverance burnished
this small vision of strangers
slowly undigging her town.

This summer a telephone repairman
sat in my kitchen in the Bronx
flirting and drinking beer and getting high
and I let him talk of anything,
of pickup softball,
of his overtime assignments,
of the time he rewired Elmira after the flood
and hung out drinking with his buddies
making bets who'd first leave town
for its stench, this old witch
who sat in a window,
any one of her seventeen cats
or these college girls who took a whole day
to unload shit from totally wasted front rooms.

The New York City World's Fairs
1939 and 1964

for my mother

We visited the World's Fair
thirteen times and saved a brochure
from every pavilion.
When you were my age then,
with a Heinz pickle pin
on a brownie collar,
you trooped through the Dawn of a New Day,
the World of Tomorrow;
marched up the Helicline
and saw Billy Rose's Aquacade.
You went back for the thrill
of stepping on a board that yelled,
"ouch, that hurts" or "don't tread on me."
GM's bright Futurama between
the Great Depression
and the Second Great War.
I put 50 cents in a machine
at the Sinclair pavilion and it produced
a fresh warm plastic dinosaur.
That was man and science—
dinosaur to oil, oil to plastic.
I wanted and got another.
You wanted to teach the family possibilities,
to show man's clever exhibitions,
but the future I came away with
was an entire house
of impermeable Formica where I wept
because my brother was lost
for the fifth time that season
and you'd gone to some hamburger-
shaped tent to pick him up again.

Stella D'Oro

In Memoriam, M.T.R., 1934–1984
Chairman, Department of English
The Bronx High School of Science

You were the freedom of the place.
Sir Isaac Newton loomed with arms outstretched
atop the mosaic pyramid of blessed
or noble scientists, our glazed muses,
and every morning, palpable and heady,
the perfume of Stella D'Oro baking
arrived from the factory and spread
its sugary call to class as we were waking.

At the vertex of the L-shaped school was built
a useless urban rooftop observatory
from which we tried to measure the planet's tilt.
One part of "L" housed formaldehyde and gory
experiments on hearts, acid fumes
and agar, rotting colonies of flies.
From that place we've cultured no one yet
who can solve the mystery of your death.

But in the other wing, always sweet
with fantasy, with anise and almond, we'd meet
Othello, Desdemona, Emma, Jude.
Anise still brings back my suspended breath,
the silent classroom as you read Macbeth's
and Lady Macbeth's whispers of Act Two,
Scene Two: "Who lies i' th' second chamber? . . ."
We jumped, all of us, terrified guilty thanes,
when, actor-pedagogue, you knocked at line
sixty-five, prelude to the porter scene.

A sun around which we revolved,
you assigned *The Explicator* and *Poetry,*
created in us small and hopeful scholars
though we were teenagers and naturally
desperate. You gave us books describing our fears.

But now time calls for turns upon the themes
of cruelty and loss and immortality.
Teacher and adviser, I want to unveil
a constellation of all the pretty words
you opened once upon a time to me.
They hover over what I teach *my* students,
waft and wait a moment in the pale
aroma of a remembered golden star.
Shakespeare, Hardy, Conrad, Forster, Yeats . . .
Everyone's of course, but also mine. And yours.
I offer them to someone else's will
and they return transformed, remain yours still.

Two Men Loved Me Once

Two men loved me once
for my long long knee-long hair.
One would sing and tell me
of an old religious man
who had declared
that only God my dear
could love Anne Gregory
for herself alone
and not her yellow hair.
The other knew a life so hard
he never shed a prayer
nor murmured out his tears
but wept, or said he wept,
to see me shorn beyond repair.
And like the foolish Anne
in front of young men in despair
I believed nothing simple or sincere.

Now and then I move my small, bare
head and feel the heft
of what's not there.

Halfway There

A smell of oranges suffused the room
and sharpened as you peeled a new one.
Beyond the window, wide views of the Hudson,
and below, the meat packers' carcasses
lined up in the foredawn having lined up
all night there . . .
                        This returns
lately as I work with women who know
your father and live that life
I over and over tried to throw
my teenaged self into.
I read Leroi Jones and felt like the woman
in the train of *Dutchman*.
Reading, reading, reading, George Jackson,
Eldridge Cleaver, Angela Davis, Richard Wright,
my sympathy evolved and opened—
a clam, a deep conch, a scaly fish, a sea urchin.
I swam it all out
and still the water met me.
I threw myself into it
and swam the lanes
of the world, as it came over me, in me,
my braid heavy, swaying, tangled
in the floats dividing the lanes.
Your neat hand corrupted itself daily
to the script of an architect
that you should make a new world
while I played "Somewhere a Place for Us" on the stereo.
Dear man, I write now, I have crossed
through to that alluvial plain
where we all gather, unequal adults,
breathing the perfume of fruit trees on the other shore.
        . . . The sediment of that other time,
the one that eddied forward, your totemic face
at the center, through the seduction

of orange oil on your fingertips, juice
in your mouth, is buried by
the slow return I have made to my familial life,
life with the tart peel gone.
What remains is a small fruit:
pale, naked, vulnerable, reduced.

Doing Time in Baltimore

In the south of the city on a cold rainy February day
we visited, deliberate tourists in the city where we lived,
the Babe Ruth Birthplace and Shrine Museum,
and the Poe grave. Not much, one nor the other,
though that day enlarges brighter each day
passing, to what seems my one happy day
in Baltimore, a day carved out against
the reduced joys of a lonely year in graduate school.

I kept Edgar and the Babe as small
icons proving the valuable universe might still swirl
from a daydream of my Bronx adolescence.
The cottage that housed Virginia Poe's last day
sat just off the Concourse. In front
was a gazebo strewn with dealers and the stuff
of their sullen art. A mile away past Krum's variety of nuts
and soda fountain, past Loews's twinkling ceiling
under which my high-school class graduated one June day
into the world, past the courthouse, the House That Ruth Built
declared itself pure white and green.

That day in Baltimore we walked a few blocks.
In the narrow row-house museum, I was dazed
to learn we could have bought a home run
(a fund raiser) to be ours forever as if
it were our own achievement.

Then, making it through each day,
as I did for two hundred and seventy days,
was achievement enough for me.
But in truth even a random single day, any day,
still is: the body's natural day
spirals out longer, contracts again and finally

rests, an old cuckoo spring pulled too far,
pulled one hour past what clocks call
when they call it a day.
A diurnal distortion we live in,
our bodies pushing out while the clocks pull in
in a struggle that becomes our dream of days.

Wall Building

At the pensione in Rome
the older Neapolitan couple
and their nine-year-old Lolita
chatted with the slurred tones of dialect,
moss and wild grass growing
from the careful plan of their words.
How young I was to teach in university,
how old to be unmarried.
The headaches I imagined, speaking Italian·
with my friend whose plans involved
marriage and life with his family.
Saltless Florentine bread.
"You would become an Italian wife, sweetheart.
I like '*sweet heart*' because it translates."
A wall of headaches, stone by stone
of every misunderstanding,
and the middle language itself
what was between us.

When my conversation partner said mildly,
"We do not travel so much in summer;
two years ago my husband had a stroke"
and widened her eyes to say,
"He cannot talk" I imagined
waking up suddenly to a man of such silence,
like trying to find the gate in a wall
familiar only from another direction.
My wall on different territory,
what my friend never saw as incongruous—
the morning after we met the Neapolitan
he arrived at breakfast smiling at me
with an Italian wave.

Opening and closing both hands,
fingers to palms facing him,
all backwards to my eyes,
he repeated the only English salutation he knew—
Goodbye! Goodbye! Goodbye!

The Monk and the Udāyana Statue of Buddha

Rings and rings of sandalwood formed
concentric. The image of Buddha Buddha approved.
By day Chōnen carried the Udāyana image through
the Himalayas. Mountain passes, long elliptical clouds.
At night a gold foil moon
lit the statue's way as it carried
the tired monk riding its back
like an awkward child playing horsie on a tall father.
A parable of rigid strength turned flexible.
A parable of Monk Chōnen, that thoughtful
workhorse, taught rewards for dedication,
taught elliptical lessons in reincarnation.
To what compare their summer's journey?
Return to the scroll
where life is a great orderly plan, gives
such a generous perspective as to seem surreal.
Over time we see the breadth of impossible order
while any one moment of chaos
is true. After movement rests order.
And it is not in time that we precede time.
This line of verse says one nothing
and this that tonight lonely I miss you. So too,
that turbulent mountain eddy and that grimace,
together, the lines combine.
The lush spill of waterfall holds
the stone bridges, and this Emaki narrative scroll
tells me that one day you, and I too, lucky us,
will have our tired feet lifted into Buddhist clouds.

"The Wild Brother to Whose Hand of Power
The Great Lioness Stalks, Purring"

Against the swelling of a day,
a Balinese woman's light pressure
above her husband's breastbone
brings syncope and sleep and dreams
of where the earth is flat and moist and rich,
where he moves across a growing field
with ease in any direction.
But the woman's memory, awake
in that part of the night
where time and energy and mass gather
to a field of gravity, loops her back
to childhood, to fruits soft with rot,
toward an old age generations away
where skin stays perfectly smooth
over the ripple of muscle and nerve,
and later loops her back,
still in her husband's arms,
to that time before she knew to know
herself in future or in miniature,
to the first sight of a turtle
swollen and upturned on the edge of sand,
stopped utterly from the brown fury
of its muddled, moonlit machinations.

The Fruition of Berneray, Hebrides

Kate Dix speaks of the boat

.

"Because they were hearing noises
    like striking with a hammer and also seeing
    a light down in the middle thwart
    but, when they got up close, was nothing there,
    they said they'd not go out in her again
    and sold the boat to Angus son of Ian
    who said he did not think a thing of it.

"A woman who had left the island was at
    the poorhouse. Nothing but black wood coffins there.
    When word arrived that she had gone,
    Angus and Norman in the *Fruition* went out
    and put the coffin on the thwart
    on which the light was. Norman dressed the box
    with tassels and stuff to make her decent
    for going under sod. In all years since
    no light, no striking, nothing has happened yet.

"*I've* heard the fairies, but not like keeps the poor-
    house woman safe. And so I'm going to tell
    how old I am since none is hearing me.
    Eighty-eight and eighty-nine July
    if I am spared. We are three with me in age—
    Katherine, daughter of Norman, and Mary, nurse.
    We were together always and we are
    together in the same year, watching lights
    for they will tell, by glowing or by dark,
    what we have left—the mischief of the life
    or the play protecting what will go."

From the Diary of Juan de Pareja

Mulatto Assistant to Diego Velázquez

Madrid, March 1631

The sun, streaming in our atelier,
reflected by pale palace stones,
washes the color of Spanish skin.
Señora Calderón forgets this, worshipping
her face in the mirror.
"Ivory is what I am—
smooth, white, firm. Be careful
with the paints!"

Working early,
I'm alone with shadows
of people frozen in studies as I stretch
canvasses, grind pigments
in silence.
This morning she arrived early, assaulting me
with her chatter while we waited for Diego
to come and convert her, too,
flat and mute on his easel.

Naples, July 1649

Here no twitch
of mine goes
unnoticed.
Watched by
the second:
my eyelid
sweeping
across the eye,
I'm one man
walled in
smoky glass.

Florence, November 1649

Italy is lonely. Diego finds his pleasure
in the cities, each day tracking their treasures,
perhaps a dried and carved band of bone
to glide on fingers glittering with stones.
I follow after him weighed down with papers
and sketches, rush to catch his cape
as he flicks it off his shoulder.
I tell him stories of my mother
as fragile and expensive as any goddess
we might bring back for King Philip to caress.

Nights, I imagine my father, that dark Moor,
coming to the rose, the jewel, the whore,
my mother in Seville's alley streets. He deserved
her no more than Philip does the curved
tiara we bought. No more than I deserve this.
Always an artist's servant, doing less
than I can do, I will never see
my studio at court or be sent to Italy
with my stipend and furs, trailing
a blacker puppy at my tail.

Rome, January 1650

In this excitement before Diego
begins his portrait of Pope Innocent
he's painting mine. It's his
exercise and a gift
for my loneliness; but an image
that reminds of self
is no gift and no remedy either
for aches and longing.

This canvas square is so much my likeness
that people no longer address me,
expecting the voice to come from the painting.
Already more of me lies in the oily ridges
of that stretched fabric
than in all my living body. Amazed,
I've watched Diego touch
my soul, seal it in plaster,
his love tormenting me from the wall.

Madrid, February 1661

Tolerated here, in Diego's empty studio,
I'm permitted to continue. In my
"Calling of Saint Matthew" I paint myself

a lesser figure in the corner. True, I've made
my skin lighter, altogether less
black than my real mulatto.

One's art and children serve identical purposes;
a son is nothing more than a self-portrait.
As my muddy father took mother for his medium,

my creation shapes a paler child
not wholly unlike myself and, with
his European nose, much improved.

Madrid, March 1661

Old Señora Calderón was here this morning
with her daughter. Unaware of Diego's death
they came for a marriage portrait.
We agreed I'd do it "providing
you learned, while in Italy, to imitate
the alabaster of their cathedrals in women's tones."
If I loved her daughter as Diego loved me
I'd search for her heart and use it to shape
the figure, but what I wanted more
was to throw her on the floor and take her.
As I shaded the face,
the pigments of her skin became blacker
than coal and her nose lay flat against
her face like a squashed pear.

That First Angelico

Gorgeous light gorgeously lit.
Palpable brilliance pushed me away
from the vases of roses, her embroidered hem,
the knees of her lap thrust forward,
from the composition carefully built,
its cool blues and cool pinks balanced,
a rich red in throne, crown, pomegranate core,
from that construct of man and saint and angel
all exploded by light.
Angel gowns seared, the child's polished forehead
like a brass censer,
there was nothing so brilliant since
as that first discovery that I could be thrown back,
not as looking into the sun
will hurt the eyes,
but because light has its own order;
it touches the breast
and then the backs of the shoulders and draws you in,
because that light like a patient lover
builds a room and holds you there
at arms' distance to admire, warm, ready
and slowly pulls you till skin is no longer skin,
painted surface not that, till you too are glowing
and you hardly know what with.

Departure

I

In the long hall of a four-hundred-
year-old museum, curtains pulled,
tapestries absorbing
the very last light and the languid
shuffle of custodians at seven,
no one brings light or conversation,
no one troubles to note the disappointment
of the regular, of the missing miracle,
of the fact that what we saw coming, from far off,
or not coming, was correct.

II

At the airport on the outskirts of a nearby town
the one plane a day each day empties its passengers
and takes the new ones waiting in the prefab terminal.
It can be so late, the tarmac and the parking lot
and the harvested fields seen
from a muddy slope behind the corrugated building
suspend in a shimmering heat of possibility.

III

With its muslin dullness the logical occurs
most often. And the sensible world proceeds.
The plane arrives. All the travelers—the eager,
the tired, the reluctant, and the tearful—
enter and fly away.

IV
The statue of the biblical warrior,
at whose base they met each evening,
doesn't change though she has left the city.
The figure's fixed stone strength persists
even if he can't deliver up the beloved.
Touched with rain and pigeons
his heroics, set into his tense neck,
do not soften or relax; and so
become the stuff of dailiness which requires
that though the story be told as often
as the lover passes beneath his vacant gaze,
though it be told one hundred times as often,
the warrior never be murdered by Evil
so that the ordinary, its own kind
of evil, everywhere triumphs.

Letter to a Milder Winter

I brought back the weather of your city
that city known for its taciturn and moody
people in whom I found reluctant, more
trustworthy friends.
Each dark eight-in-the-morning the river
beneath my window rushed like pouring rain
and I might have slept the long tucked-in
inclement day,
the sky, by half hours, moving from dark
to light to hazed to clear.
These sadnesses now: wet thoughts
or the nostalgic gold of five
minutes of morning clearing over palazzi.
By the window I absorbed it—
each dramatic change.
The cloud which began of very little
suddenly a sponge of all the weather,
substance enough to rain, to overshadow,
to drift, to drift, to drift.

The Block in Summer

for Sara and Ellis

We tried lemonade sales because we'd seen
them done on television.
We sat in the gutter, grinding silver rocks
we would refine, waiting for them to pan out
literally, that was the scheme,
until we confronted the irrefutable existence of mica.
We played stoop with a spall-deen.
We put on productions of fairy tales and *West Side Story*.
We traded records, toys and books
in a circular flea market.
Ice-cream trucks came up and down
and played lucky number with us.
We lay struggling toward both peaces,
sleep and awake, lone fish flapping
on dry ground in our beds
beside windows, while grownups talked.

All afternoon we'd hear
from the west the IRT rumble by
and from the east the deep bellow
of Freedomland's steamship.
First one, then a little bit later, the other.
The city settled down
on a slowly rocking seesaw
to the two sounds,
the IRT train and the ship whistle,
growing louder.
On lucky nights, cuddled in my father's
lap, lime rickeys with Fox's raspberry all
around, I'd fall asleep among folding chairs
listening for the deep resonant reassurance
that our Freedomland was still there.

Led by the Hebrew School Rabbi

Those good students, who only loved working
through pages of exercises,
but were too good to object to the philanthropy
of physical recreation, took a bus
to the Grand Concourse and another one down it,
modelled after the Champs Elysées in Paris France,
to the aging YMHA by Yankee Stadium.

We stumbled on the basketball court
of that cavernous decrepit building
flapping like ducks, but outran the Yeshiva boys'
whose tzitzis, even to us, were ridiculous,
a sign of obvious distress and incompetence.

In the pool, girls and boys segregated
across the olympic length,
we didn't know what to do.
Nothing we could figure out.
Confused. Nothing we could read.
In rubber caps we floated and ducked,
white knots of feathers drifting in the musty steam.

Samuel

As soon as I knew all the verses of the Shema
by heart they pushed me to my grandfather where he sat
so I could recite them.
The year before, I'd dropped belly to floor
in my velvet dirndl,
arched, and touched toes to head repeatedly
while the Family Circle admired my gymnastics.
He had just unwrapped the phylacteries;
the slight red depressions crossing his arm
were rising and receding. He was reading the psalms.
I said, "v'awhavtaw ais hashem . . . chirp chirp chirp . . .
polly want a cracker? . . . uv'lecht'chaw baderech,
uv'shawchb'chaw . . ."
All three paragraphs, rapid fire, including,
in the third, kissing, as if a man, my imaginary tallis.
And he nodded, gave no praise or smile,
only the silent shame that this piece of faith
was not performable, that the covered eyes
and whispered declarations come in fear,
humility and concentration. I had made a mistake.
He showed me the cavern I might fall into.
I would fall over and over.
His namesake anointed Saul and warned Saul
of the future history of his devastating pride.
Quiet and diligent in his habits
of which his observance was composed,
my grandfather found prayer like the constant weather
of a mild American June,
no Galician struggle
with the rightness, perfection, presentation,
correction of what the Lord has given.
Just—when He calls: "Here am I."
And when He asks: "I have heard and I will do."
"I accept" simply taken unto peace and unto life.

Orcio and Fiasco

The flat underbellied fish-shaped scar on his forehead,
imprinted as if a fossil were imbedded and bleached
there, asked for explanation, to be read.

His text began with his car and the fish bucket he reached
out to to keep upright through a sharp curve
that sent him swerving over the road's edge into the breach

of terraced olive groves and vineyards that serve
in this utilitarian landscape for systems of heaven and hell,
the graded charts and maps that still preserve

the mnemonic fidelity of the Divine Comedy, as well
as the frescoes which derive from it, as living documentary.
And the Lord put a Fiat Cinquecento on those Tuscan hills

crashing with the logic of the Road Runner or Bugs Bunny.
A bucket, muddy water, worms, all the tackle, all the fish
flying separately through the car as the car flew. An elementary

physics film illustrating the first moment of undiminished
movement, lines and arrows, trajectory of water, momentum,
acceleration, vectors, gravity the same as in the Pisan parish.

Or it might be fear animate in a many-panelled pastel cartoon
of objects tumbling in energetic spirals skewed
into a chaos of crosses, stars and expletives, suns and moons.

Either way—approximate emotive sketches that won't hurt you
or compass-precise diagrams—neither one is the truth and both
just describe a human order we insinuate upon divine virtue.

Herschel's Milk

James Stephen Gibert Yarrow

How much water in the world,
how mutable.
This might be the first lesson, or that seventy-nine
percent of our bodies are water
and never mind the remainder, the few cents'
worth of chemicals. Understand I mean
to imply that vague popular correlation
with the percentage of water on earth.
And let me mention salt-water tears
right now. And move on.
But let us dwell on how you came
to cheer me: "I saw the White Horse
of the Vale in the clouds."
We will never know what you meant
in your dreamy child's meditation;
if it is true or
how much true. It certainly can't
mean those primitive white chalk
lines of earthwork, but instead
I think the strong white flesh
of the various pub signs you saw.

That you (that any of us) knew at once
that "going to Bath" would not be a cleansing experience
is only barely clear because the Romans
—you got your Roman Soldier Book—
and also Jane Austen and also others took baths
of a kind there. The streets of the town are dry
but the Baths were wet and steamy
and sulfurous. You posed like a patient narcissist
for nearly every picture,
dangling over the algaed water of the pools
or passing your arm across the sea-creatures mosaics,
but wouldn't approach the great rush of steam
pouring from the excavation, the dangerous
mouth of the universe.

60

We visited the houses of two dogged men,
impeccable George Saintsbury
and the man who, serving tea and playing the spinet,
saw way out beyond this blue blue globe.
In his house, solemn-eyed and gently
holding my hand, you stepped up to the telescope
while the guide, an anxious if lonely member
of the Herschel Society,
explained methods of grinding lenses.
As you murmured, "yes, I see,"
I felt I'd sailed the generous seas of time.

We were in Bath and I thought about holding
you four years before—before and after
you were christened in an Oxford chapel
where I recalled that Hannah's tears
made her seem liquid drunk in the Temple.
I thought in Bath about the kettles steaming all over England,
the steam of the old trains charging all across England,
and the water moving all above England
in clouds falling as rain covering all England,
the green green jewel.

The liquid commerce of love, sitting down
to tea and more tea
for years with your mother
until finally we found ourselves talking
about you, who knew only such love as in milk.
The bottle of milk with a red cap
at Herschel's doorstep, nineteen New King Street,
was it Herschel's milk? you asked,
or was it the Romans'? or the Vikings'?
They say milk is the perfect food,
is water mixed with, made from, life.

Perhaps a life from that planet
I wish for you to discover, see, visit.
"*He* used to retire to bed with a basin
of milk or a glass of water;
with Smith's *Harmonics* or Ferguson's *Astronomy*
and so went to sleep buried."
Whose milk was it, small cool and white
hesitating on the doorstep of the private museum.
Your dilemma. Should you bring it in or let it rest
on the surface of the earth for him
to somehow recover and let us, somehow, recover ourselves.

About the Author

Judith Baumel has been director of the Poetry Society of America since 1985.

Baumel is a graduate of Radcliffe College, Harvard University (B.A. 1977) and The Writing Seminars of The Johns Hopkins University, where she received an M.A. in 1978. She won a 1987 poetry fellowship from the New York Foundation for the Arts and the Lloyd McKim Garrison Medal for Poetry. She has been lecturer at Harvard University, Boston University, and the City College of New York. Her home is in New York City.

About the Book

The Weight of Numbers was composed in Garamond #3 by G&S Typesetters of Austin, Texas, and printed and bound by Arcata Graphics/Kingsport of Kingsport, Tennessee. The design is by Kachergis Book Design & Production, Inc. of Pittsboro, North Carolina.

Wesleyan University Press, 1988